Bridge Over Troubled Waters

By

Gregory L. Grose

AuthorHouse™
1663 Liberty Drive
Bloomington, IN 47403
www.authorhouse.com
Phone: 1 (800) 839-8640

Published by AuthorHouse 06/05/2015

ISBN: 978-1-4184-2759-7 (sc)

Library of Congress Control Number: 2004092136

Print information available on the last page.

This book is printed on acid free paper.

Table of Contents

> INTRODUCTION

I suspect, that like me, many black youths are growing up in the shadows of American society trying to make sense of a world they despise, and a world they perceive despises them. They come from broken homes and shattered dreams, where the lives they lead do not measure up to the standards of mainstream society. With little more than splinters of hope to cling to, these youths scratch desperately against the despair of their lives, searching for themselves in a myriad of distorted images created from their own denial of truth. They are victims of misinformation and sub-education, and consequently, they are slaves to delusion arising from a life of lies (2 Thessalonians 2:11).

I remain determined to sound the alarm, and give warning in our time that Jesus Christ stands at the door and knocks — let Him in! This is our last chance to save our communities from the moral decay that has spread like a new strain of hopelessness, frustrating our approach to God. Jesus the Christ is the final bridge, in a long journey, which every human soul must cross in order to find rest. He stands with outstretched arms and open hands beckoning us, "Come to me, all you who are weary and carry heavy burdens, and I will give you rest" (Mathew 11:28, NLT).

God has moved in my spirit to write, *Bridge Over Troubled Waters*. It is here that we can begin to understand some of the more perplexing problems in life, and find a bridge to cross from the problem to the promise.

This book is my desperate attempt to address the gulf that stands at the crux of all our problems, and finds its expression in violence and crime, war and famine, power and lust.

I am certain that many of the issues in this book will be controversial, and no doubt raise the ire of those who have invested in traditional perspectives for understanding the crisis in human affairs. For that reason I have been careful to support my findings by the Word of God (2 Timothy 3:16).

The thesis of this book is simply this: the gulf that stands between God and man explains most if not all of the violence and crime plaguing our communities. Only by understanding the role of Jesus Christ can we be equipped adequately to deal with those problems, and erect a bridge to traverse the gap that separates us from God.

The implication of my thesis is somewhat staggering, for what I am suggesting flies in the face of traditional wisdom, that looks to contemporary sociological perspectives for an explanation concerning the escalation of violence and crime in our cities. I suggest that psychology, sociology, and criminology are inadequate for effectively explaining the ills that ravage the Black community. "For the weapons of our warfare *are* not carnal but mighty in God for the pulling down of strongholds" (2 Corinthians 10:4, NKJV).

My thesis further suggests that the Black community has witnessed staggering increases in crimes of violence perpetrated by and against youth, because of the spiritual gulf that stands at the core of their cultural life. Emancipation and Civil Rights has brought us to the dinner table of America, but in the wake of laying hold of America's most prized possessions we have neglected to make spiritual growth a primary focus for directing our lives. Thus, we have given birth to a generation of people with unhealthy appetites, who lust after every perverse pleasure known to man.

I pray that by the time you finish this book, you will have gained a greater urgency for the spreading of the Gospel, and a renewed appreciation for the spiritual legacy that forms the backbone of our cultural strivings. Additionally, that you begin to realize that the Christian life must amount to more than moaning and groaning of old battle hymns on Sunday morning. But rather, our life should be a beacon of hope in communities that have all but died of spiritual starvation.

Finally, I hope that you gain a greater appreciation for the Word of God, and begin to allow the word of life to minister to your every need. So that in the midst of hopelessness you might see Jesus Christ as the bridge over troubled waters.

1 > Testimony Of The Saints

Come *and* hear, all you who fear God, And I will declare what He has done for my soul.

Psalms 66:16 (NKJV)

And they overcame him by the blood of the Lamb and by the word of their testimony; and they did not love their lives to the death.

Revelation 12:11 (NKJV)

When we have traveled the meandering roads of time, and have found ourselves exhausted by the daily grind of life, the one thing that matters most in the end is, "What does it all mean?" That is the proverbial question that has occupied some of the greatest minds in history, and has stirred in the heart of all but the most benighted souls.

I believe the answer to that question is revealed to us somewhere between Christ's demonstration of love for us and David's declaration of faith in God. For when David looked back over both the terrible and merciful works of God, he could not but utter one resounding cry: "...I will declare what He has done for my soul" (Psalms 66:16, NKJV). That is the one realization that spells the difference between a life lived in pursuit of vain desires and a life spent seeking after all that God is. The one leads to an endless search for things that never fill us nor stops the insatiable yearning that lives at the center of our existence. The other, as David discovered, answers the cry of the human soul.

The words of David's testimony comes down to us through the echoes of time, and when we are almost faint from the burdens of our life God's act of love renews our staggering hope. Just when it looks like Satan has won the war with a crushing maneuver to our blind side, we "overcame him by the blood of the Lamb" (Revelation 12:11, NKJV). Put another way, when the weight of Satan's attacks seem to be wearing us down, it is the act of Jesus Christ's saving grace that brings us back into the palace of God's favor.

Do not make the mistake of cheapening the sacrifice Jesus made at the Cross, as if our victory over Satan awaits some later act to be performed by Jesus' second coming. Jesus has already given us authority and the power to defeat the enemy

(Mathew 28:18; Luke 10:19). Through the life that is in Christ Jesus we become *letters* "… written in our hearts, known and read of all men" (2 Corinthians 3:2, NKJV). It is the expression of our transformed lives that bears witness, before a wicked and perverse generation, that Jesus Christ is the final answer to the central question of life. But until we can stand before the courtroom of the world and confess that Jesus is Lord, we can have no real power over Satan's control of our lives. That is why Jesus said, " If anyone acknowledges me publicly here on earth, I will openly acknowledge that person before my Father in heaven. But if anyone denies me here on earth, I will deny that person before my Father in heaven" (Mathew 10:32-33, NLT).

Our public confession of Christ is our testimony. It is a social act of boldness that ushers from the throne of God the promise of His protection even "to the death" (Revelation 12:11b, NKJV). For within the social context of our expression of God's goodness we find encouragement and strength through listening to the testimony of others and expressing our own (Wade, 2003, p.8). In Malachi 3:16 (KJV), the people that feared the Lord spoke of him among themselves with heart-felt reverence, and the Lord "heard *it*, and a book of remembrance was written before him…"

God's demonstration of love (the blood of the Lamb) is our justification before the throne of grace and our declarations of faith (the word of our testimony) are our sanctification before the court of the world. So that in our final walk through the shadow of death we will have escaped the holds of fear over our lives, and ultimately, like Enoch of old, walk with God!

I believe that the Word of God is true, infallible, and the reliable wellspring from which the mysteries of life are uncovered. The Apostle Peter writes that the word did not originate from man, but came to special men of old "as *they were* moved by the Holy Spirit" (2 Peter 1:21, NKJV). The Word is like beads strung together in one harmonious cord, each separate but part of the whole. It is a *progressive doctrine*, that is, "truths or teachings which appear in…earlier parts of scriptures are found to have recurring mention and developing build-up right through the Bible" (Baxter, 1985, p. 20). At each successive stage, through each historical period, book after book, page after page, God is tying together His ultimate plan for man. Then somewhere amid the historical stage of time we come unto the scene with our own biographical ties to both the old and the new, and shatter the silence of obscurity with our testimony.

A Child Seeing God

When I look back over my life I am struck by the sequel of events that led me to God, and ultimately to the place where I am now. So here is my testimony.

Like David, "I will declare what He [God] has done for my soul" (Psalms 66:16, NKJV emphasis mine)!

I accepted Jesus Christ as my Lord and Savior in 1971, at the impressionable age of 11. I could not know then how the sequence of events would sweep me from the protective halls of Lutheran Children's Friend Society to the security halls of Green Correctional Institution. Neither could I understand how the hand of God was holding death at bay while the path for my salvation was being forged from the debris of my past. But glancing back some 30 or more years I can not help but marvel at all the miracles and wonders He wrought in my life.

There I was at age seven, beneath the blistering sun with a few of my neighborhood friends, hammering on bullets with a brick, as the deafening sound of the bullet exploded in the air. For a brief moment in time I imagined that I, like Superman, could dodge bullets with the speed of light. So with precision and ease I attempted to dart through the path of the speeding bullet as it exploded in the air directly in front of me. But as the metal met my stomach all I knew was the intense sting of heat, and the crescendo of mixed sounds and hazy images that shock filtered in. I awoke in the County Hospital somewhat oblivious to what had happened, only now looking back can I see the hand of God.

In 1970 I was sent to a group home called the Lutheran Children's Friend Society. I suppose my mother, with four other children to raise, could no longer muster the strength to deal with my worsening behavior, that had gotten so bad that I was down to a half a day in school.

I spent the next three years in the Lutheran home learning to mask what I felt, and in the grips of my own isolation I learned to escape from the world at the point of a pencil. I began to write stories about far away lands where I was king and all was grand, and children lived happily ever after. But in the real world I was filled with rage, and an almost impulsive urge to strike out where I could, often ending my day being physically restrained by one of the counselors at the group home.

I guess I wasn't much different from a thousand other black boys that struggled with feelings of abandonment and low self-esteem, growing up in a time when America was redefining who she was.

Have you ever looked into an old man's face and traced the lines that etch their story across his battered skin? Ever wonder why he stares out at the world with such rapt composure and such loss? I believe like me, he stands on the edge of time and marvels at the sheer genius of a Creator who neglects nothing. He has weathered some storms, and seen the sun gather itself over the horizon for another trek across the belly of the sky as it has done numerous times before. At some deeper level he has seen God through the eyes of a child. What wonder! What grace!

I seen God through the eyes of child when I was 11 years old, having accepted Jesus Christ and been baptized in the customary Lutheran tradition. I remember sitting in a classroom at Our Redeemer Lutheran School, designated for the children at Lutheran Children's Friend Society. God touched my heart so irresistibly, that from somewhere within the deep recesses of my soul I felt His love, and being so moved and enraptured I created a felt banner. I cut out the shape of a world, a house, and a heart. I positioned them on that felt banner, coining the words: *God Comes Into Your World Into Your Home Into Your Heart.* Shortly thereafter I appeared on channel 36, when evangelistic programming was still popular on Sunday mornings. I don't know if it was the novelty of the banner that brought me to television or whether the seventies was a time to showcase black folks as a liberal demonstration of faith. But what I do know now is that God was even then shaping who I would ultimately become.

I believe that God's providential will for us is present from the time we take our first breath until the time we ultimately accept him. For God is "not willing that any should perish but that all should come to repentance" (2 Peter 3:9, NKJV), and the intervening time in our lives is just his "longsuffering" or grace. God is shaping the whole of our life, and if we miss the mark it is only our unwillingness to be shaped that condemns us. Why else would God send Jeremiah down to the potter's house, then declare to His people, "Look, as the clay *is* in the potter's hand, so you *are* in My hand, O house of Israel" (Jeremiah 18:6, NKJV)! Apostle Paul understood this when he wrote to the Romans. "We are assured *and* know that [God being a partner in their labor] all things work together *and* are [fitting in a plan] for good to *and* for those who love God and are called according to [His] design and purpose" (Romans 8:28, Amp).

From that theological perspective the word of our testimony takes on added weight, and must be regarded as more than the emotionless recitals of accidental events of people stumbling into salvation. Rather, our testimonies become the lively confessions of believers who are awed by the love of a God that never sleeps nor slumbers as he passes us from grace to glory.

If you have never been a child growing up on the black side of America you might think it strange that a little boy like me could grow up not knowing who he was. Had you not heard your love ones call you that "black ugly so and so," you might not understand my distorted image of life, where everything white was cuddly and nice and everything black was bad. Perhaps by the time that ugly little boy had made his way to school he was angry and hostile, spitting on teachers and beating up the other children who had nothing to do with the pain he felt. And maybe those secret things that happened to him, when he was a child, made him prisoner to emotions he could not understand nor find the words to express.

Out Of Place

I was released from the Lutheran Children's Friends Society in 1973. During my stint at the group home I had been to two private schools, and was presently in the seventh grade at Holy Ghost Lutheran School. But something happened to me that set the tone for the next 23 years of my life. When I arrived back into the black community, still struggling to make sense of who I was and how I fit into life, I was met by what can only be described as the backlash of racial insecurity. For one day I was hanging out with some of the neighborhood boys, supposedly some of the coolest guys on the block, and as soon as I began to speak, with all the marks of proper education, someone in the crowd quipped, "Hey! He talk like a white boy!" The next few moments after that were filled with laughter and the crushing sound that silent egos make when death has visited their shores.

I can not adequately explain what happened to me in those moments, only that I spent the next 23 years struggling to reconcile my distorted concept of self with the realities of my race's cultural insecurities and fears.

Those fears have not disappeared, and continue to fuel traditional talks about race relations. We are fond at pointing out the systematic injustices that continue to be obstacles to our race, but there is an unspoken rule that prevents us from looking at ourselves, and allows the disease of our own destruction to go untreated. But perhaps that is due in part to a residual fear that has outlasted the changing canvass of Black America, a fear of appearing naked and vulnerable before a world that is perceived to be painted white.

By January 1976 I was sent to Ethan Allen School for Boys, a boys reformatory, for 19 months.

By 1982 my whole world came crashing down as I stood before the judge, just beyond the questioning eyes of accusers and friends. For that instant justice removed her blind long enough to look upon 135 pound black native, left at the mercy of a system touted to remedy the wrongs committed against society.

"Ten years for robbery to run concurrent with 20 years for second degree murder to run consecutive to 20 years...." The judge's voice trailed off into the abyss as he passed the 70-year sentence. In those moments all I could mange to do was recoil back inside myself, numbed by the denial of a reality that I had learned to twist upon itself, until all that remained was a distorted lie to fit my version of truth.

The next 10 years in prison were spent battling to come to grips with the crimes I had committed and the person I had become. Even now as I look back I scarcely recognize the stranger that stares back accusingly in the mirror. We seem to have little in common, and were it not for the residual effects of my anger and hate I would have all but forgotten his name. I was sure I had managed to bury him some years ago when I had dunned the name Omar Shadeed Muhammad. I thought prayer five times a day, fasting 30 days once a year, strict dietary regiments, and learning the Arabic language would be enough to lay hold of a future that would free me from my past. The harder I tried to escape who they said I was, echoes of that "ugly black boy" still pounding in my head, the more angry I became at the prospect of it all being true.

I guess what attracted me to the Islamic religion was its underlying defiance of Western culture, for after all, I had come to believe that it was the white man that had ravaged my race, and gave birth to the conditions that were responsible for my own hopelessness.

The Muslims taught me familiar stories about Abraham, Isaac, and Jacob. I have to admit that the most difficult doctrine for me to reconcile was that of Jesus Christ. Had they directly slandered Jesus their proselytizing would have never swayed me. But they did something more insidious, they denied his divinity without denying him. They even directed me to bible verses that seemed to validate their beliefs. Soon my anger consumed me, and I started to regard myself much as a political prisoner would, finally adopting the Muslim way of life in 1982.

I am convinced that when Jesus Christ made his intercessory appeal to his Father near the garden of Gethsemane (Geth-se-man-ee) it was especially for me. For he said, " I am praying not only for these disciples but also for all who will believe in me because of their testimony" (John 17:20, NLT). His words were so sublime and far-reaching that they set off a chorus in heaven, and fell like morning dew upon the genetic puzzle of my life, and covered me with God's grace. How else do you explain a man, having spent eight years practicing the Muslim religion, a Muslim minister, law giver, leader, follower, and devout enemy of Christ, in 2003 pealing back the pages of time to unveil this testimony to Christ Jesus?

Sitting here on January 22, 2003, hammering out what perhaps is the greatest individual work that I have ever been inspired to write I am staggered by the overwhelming power of what Jesus Christ has done in my life. Even my ability to give poetic wings to the splendor of God's handiwork, would fall woefully short of capturing the sheer beauty of how this loving father has cradled me with his protective arms from birth. But inadequate as my feeble words may prove, I must, for the sake of touching some shattered spirit, that has suffered the painful stings of life, unfold the magnificence of God's work in shaping my life. To that end it is necessary that we take a trip to the *Potter's House,* to witness what manner of creation the potter is molding on the wheel.

In God's Hands

Jeremiah was directed by God to go down to the potter's house. "Then I went down to the potter's house, and there he was, making something at the wheel. And the vessel that he made of clay was marred in the hand of the potter; so he made it again into another vessel, as it seemed good to the potter to make" (Jeremiah 18:3-4, NKJV).

Here is the familiar tale of a man on a stool, groping over a potter's wheel, as he patiently fashions the moist clay into a form that will please him. Round and round the wheel moves as the clay begins to take form in the old, skilled hands of the potter. He has been at this business for a long time, so his expertise is unparalleled, and he labors tirelessly to finish the work now set before him. But sometimes, whether by an act of nature or just because of an inherent defect, the clay is damaged. Yet with the same deliberate and patient hands the potter starts the process again, until at long last he looks down on his finished work and exclaims, truly it is very good (Genesis 1:31)!

Understanding what takes place in the potter's house is key to understanding how God works with us throughout our lives on earth. We are born into this world as vessels of earth (2 Corinthians 4:7), fashioned and shaped by the circumstances of time.

But in the process of being formed we are damaged by events that have proven too devastating for us to overcome alone. It might be some childhood experience of rape or incestuous event that snatched our innocence away. It might have been a drug or alcohol craze that diminished our ability to stop using. Whatever the trauma was, it damaged us so irrevocably that nothing short of a miracle could restore us. But all the while, through every sleepless night, behind every tear, within every prison cell, laced between despair and hopelessness there is GOD! Still at the wheel, tirelessly turning us from despair to hope so that we might, with time and proper care, regain what Satan had stolen from us.

How comforting it is to know that at whatever point I find myself in life God still has me in his hands, and that no matter how hopeless the situation appears he is able to deliver me. I say this not as one who has learned to parrot the idealistic notions about a god I have heard others testify about, but because of my personal experience living in the presence of God. I say this because I went to prison with 70 years for second-degree felony murder, two counts of armed robbery, and nine separate armed robbery cases read into the record to enhance the sentence. But through feverish moments in prayer, trips to the law library, educational experiences, and most of all, the mercy of a God who never left the potter's wheel, I was released from prison on June 28, 1991, after having served only 10 years.

Who ever you are, wherever you are, and however you find yourself at this moment, remember, the Lord is still at the potter's wheel and he's working your situation out. He is not unmindful of your problems or the burdens that weigh you down, but he's perfecting in you a new spirit that will soar high above the clouds that threaten to darken your way.

While my release from prison in 1991 was a joyous occasion, unrivaled by any single event in my life, it was in some ways ironic. For although I had all the appearance of freedom I was still a prisoner to all the negative press I had bought into over the years. There I was, 31 years old, with all the unresolved issues of youth buried some where beneath the social veneer I had learned to wear with years of artful training. For there is an unspoken law in the hood that men don't cry and little boys are required to act like men, because pain is for sissies and love is a weakness reserved for women. Thus, some where between psychological examinations in youth detention, and the adult court of retributive justice, I never quite got a grip on how to deal with feelings of guilt, shame, abandonment, and pain. And it would take another 3 years of struggling to escape the jaws of drug and alcohol abuse before I would come face to face with the demons that were slowly destroying me.

In July 1994, after having tried unsuccessfully to stop abusing drugs and alcohol, I checked into De Paul Hospital. It was a 12 Step program of complete abstinence, that had as the core of its philosophy the idea that drug and alcohol abuse was a disease, and only through the regiment of working the 12 Step program could a person hope to live abstinent. For the next 90 days I attended groups, met with counselors, interacted with peers, and began the process of trying to rebuild the fallen walls of my life. It was during that time that the clouds of political change in the country had seriously begun to effect drug and alcohol treatment programs in Milwaukee. The conservative politics of Capitol Hill had swept across America with such fanfare that the average American had become fed up with treatment programs, that seemed to do little more than perpetuate an institution too expensive to justify. As a result, I was discharged from De Paul Hospital earlier than planned.

Remember, I said the Lord is still at the potter's wheel? Perhaps, what I also should have told you was that at whatever point you find yourself in life God will place a person or circumstance in your way to guide you along. That is why the Apostle Paul says, "For God knew his people in advance, and he chose them to become like his Son…" (Romans 8:29a, NKJV).

Since God planned for us to *come together* into the *form* or *image* of him, it was necessary that He set in place some universal laws that are fixed and immutable. One of those laws is that everything human is inherently social, and requires some degree of human contact in order to grow in a healthy way. Subsequently, no degree of growth in human affairs is accomplished without the direct or indirect influence of people. Whether through the process of our educational experiences or the bonding rituals that form the nucleus of our family and friends, each is marked by the law of social contacts. These laws of human sociability have given rise to the platitude that God works through people, and is further underscored by the divine act by which God saved us from sin through the human activity of His Son. For "God's children are human beings — made of flesh and blood — Jesus also became flesh and blood by being born in human form. For only as a human being could he die, and only by dying could he break the power of the Devil, who had the power of death" (Hebrews 2:14, NLT). That is why sprinkled along the trail of our sojourn through life are people and events that God has used to prod us in the right direction. Some times a friend, some times a stranger, some times an old familiar song —

merely signposts along the way to steer us home to God. But if we are not careful we'll squander much of youth missing what the Lord is trying to say to us, and soon wake up advanced in years, wishing we had been more mindful along the way.

Five Corners of Faith, an independent living home for recovering drug and alcohol abusers, was the vehicle through which I was to rediscover the legacy of my Christian roots, and the Reverend John Perry was to be one of the spiritual guides who would prove indispensable to leading me home.

The next five years would witness the awesome sweep of God's providential hand as He guided me along the potter's wheel from the smoke filled meeting rooms of the Twelve-Step Club to the ivory halls of the University of Wisconsin, where I earned a bachelors degree in Mass Communications. Through a maze of countless moments shared with people, in 12 step meetings, who had nothing to give, but their wretched experiences with the hopelessness of drug abuse — I stumbled into the Heavy Hitters, one of Milwaukee's premier 12 step groups, tired and ready to quit. But Linston Young, leader and founder of the Heavy Hitters, said something to me that forever changed my life. He said, "What you need to do is reexamine your belief system."

What! Why? I know who I am. I believe... silence following from some where only the angels were aware. So for the next four years I struggled to hold on to the shattered pieces of a belief I had long questioned. "I'm a Muslim, right?" The only response was the voice in my head and the throbbing in my heart that said, "Reexamine your belief…"

During those times I remember watching the graphic portrayal of Bishop T. D. Jakes as he thundered across the TV monitor in the Original Hair King Barbershop, and the Christian witnessing of the owner, Caree Huley and his brother Charles Huley. I remember frequently sitting there waiting to have my hair cut, mesmerized by the word of God as it flowed from the lips of Bishop Jakes. More and more God's words saturated me until there was no resistance left, and in those moments the word ministered to me new life where once there was death. Until in 1999 I accepted Jesus Christ as my Lord and Savior, and joined the ranks of a thousand other saints who had found rest in the Father's arms.

So when I look back over my life and think about the goodness of God, "I will declare what He hath done for my soul" (Psalms 66:16, NKJV)!

2 > Enemy In the Camp

He who has no rule over his own spirit is like
a city that is broken down and without walls.

Proverbs 25:28 (Amp.)

We listened in horror, on February 1, 2003,
as the news media interrupted normal programming
to announce that the Space Shuttle Columbia had
exploded 39 miles above the earth, killing seven
astronauts. That was the tragic news following
on the back of a State of the Union Address by
President Bush, which presage our intentions to
declare war on Iraq for its alleged threats to world
peace. Yet while these domestic and national events
seemed distant and distinct from each other — I
could not help noticing the hand of God weaving
together these discordant events into a commentary
on the human condition.

I believe that space exploration is an extension of man's search to pull together the puzzle of his existence. While war is the chaos from which man hopes to regain the peace which always eludes him. But however noble man's efforts prove they seem to fall woefully short of his aim, and in the end he is left to exclaim, "Vanity of vanities; all *is* vanity" (Ecclesiastes 1:2, NKJV). For man is trapped by the finality of his condition, and dependent on things outside his ability to control. Thus, he is subject to the limitations of his own *humanity,* and cannot escape the contradictions tied to that fact. So he tries to bring about peace by war, life by death, love by hate, and an endless barrage of senseless activities that always end in pain. But at the core of all existence goes the proverbial question of life: *"What does it all mean?"*

Solomon is known as the wisest man that ever lived. At the crossroads of his life he was faced with the decision that confronts us all, whether to settle for the immediate gain within his reach or set his gaze on the more lasting accomplishments of time. Solomon chose an understanding heart that would allow him to determine good and bad, and the ability to judge God's people (1 Kings 3:9). He chose the favor of God over the natural impulse of human nature, which clings, to things that satisfy the flesh while robbing the spirit of life. That is why

David was able to observe the nature of man when he said, "You love evil more than good and lies more than truth" (Psalms 52:3, NLT).

While knowledge and understanding can bring us closer to God, it can also draw us further from him. Thus, Solomon learned that the human appetite can hardly be tamed once it has been allowed to savor sin. Thus, "The eye is not satisfied with seeing, nor the ear filled with hearing" (Ecclesiastes 1:8, NKJV).

It is the separation from God that man is striving to reconcile with his endless and misguided feats of control. Therefore, in the end we must all find a bridge that will traverse the gap created from our own deception.

This book sets forth the thesis that the separation between God and man explains most if not all of the violence and crime plaguing our communities. Only by understanding the role of Jesus Christ can we be equipped adequately to deal with those problems, and erect a bridge over the gap that separates us from God.

Hutchinson wrote a particularly caustic article in 1999, in which he accused many black ministers across America of remaining silent while laws were passed to destroy affirmative action and weaken civil liberties (Hutchinson, 1999, p.1). He also alleged that many black churches had remained silent on cuts in health care, disparities in the criminal justice system, deterioration of public education, and a host of other social and political abuses that "left many African-Americans politically confused, socially stunted and physically at risk" (Hutchinson, 1999, p.1). Jones found that blacks were about "six times more likely than whites to be admitted to prison during their life" (Jones, 2000, p.1).

There seems to be some consensus on the fact that African Americans make up a disproportionate number of those incarcerated across the United States, and that in "the midst of [the] current boom, black unemployment persists at a discouragingly high rate. In 1995 the black male unemployment rate — 10.6 percent — was nearly twice as great as the overall unemployment rate 5.6 percent" (Schwartzman, 1997, p.1). That notwithstanding, all but the most inane apologist must admit that there is something dangerously wrong in the black community, and if we do not begin by having an open dialogue that honestly addresses those problems an entire generation will be lost.

While I admit that there are still some serious racial inequalities that frustrate and debilitate blacks in cities across America — the root of our problem does not stop at the steps of the White House — it starts and stops with us! It starts by looking at the fact that homicide is the number one cause of death for young black men, and the number two cause of death for young black women, between the ages of 15 and 24 (Simmons, 2002, p.1). In the State of Wisconsin, in the year 2000, 37 percent of homicide victims were between the ages of 14 and 24, and 60 percent of all homicide victims were black, compared to about 39 percent for whites (BJS, 2003, p.1). Blacks are six times more likely to be killed than whites, and 94 percent of blacks killed between 1976 and 1999 were killed by other black Americans (Simmons, 2002, p.1). The Wisconsin Department of Public Information reports that over half of the black high school students between grades 9 through 12 dropped out of school in the 1999-2000 school year (DPI, 2001, p.1).

I apologize if this analysis of black America embarrasses some black leaders, who continue to play on the racial sensitivities of our race, as they offer up sacrifices not meet for repentance. It is time for the truth to shatter the lies of the "black" conspiracy that wants us to believe that the condition of our communities is solely a result of powers beyond our control. That we are some how victims of some elaborate experiment that has its roots in slavery, or better still, unwitting pawns in an American game that has as its end the total annihilation of the race.

I will not remain silent while the ignorance and shame of a benighted leadership sits idly by as young black brothers and sisters snatch the breath from each other's body with little or no regard. But I, like Jude, "earnestly contend for the faith which was once for all delivered to the saints" (Jude 1:3, NKJV). For I love my people and I yet hold out hope that God is birthing new leaders, who will not be swayed by riches or sell out the cause for acceptance into favored circles. But like the Apostle Paul I will live for Christ's work or die trying to defend it (Philippians 1:21).

I believe that many of the children growing up in the shadows of American society are trying to make sense of a world they don't understand. They are trying desperately to form meaningful attachments by which to anchor themselves to life. But they are often discouraged by the limitations imposed on them by competing cultural structures that are often at odds with each other. For on the one hand, there is the dominant American culture that imposes its set of standards on them, and on the other hand, they must learn to simultaneously negotiate the subtle differences of their own culture. It is no wonder that those African-Americans that have managed to successfully negotiate between the two cultures, having attained a certain level of social standing in mainstream society, feel alienated and overcome by feelings of uncertainty and guilt. For in no small way adaptation to one culture is a *sell-*

out to the other. "You cannot serve God and money" (Mathew 6:24, NLT). Perhaps that is why many black youths spend enormous amounts of energy searching for themselves in a myriad of distorted images no matter how perverse or obnoxious. That might help to explain the godlike appeal of young rap singers, who snub their noses at traditional mores, while celebrating drugs, sex, and death. But while I do not agree with those who suppose that rap music is the *cause* of crime; I do see rap music as an expression of our desperation and uncertainty over life, and a clear indication that we have lost control of spiritual values that once gave us pause. The wall of morality that helped to shape our lives from the slave fields of Mississippi to the picket lines of Alabama have been torn down, and in the wake of peace and love many of us have opted for war and hate. But be forewarned, "Whoever *has* no rule over his own spirit *Is like* a city broken down, without walls (Proverbs 25:28, NLT).

Communities Under Attack

Like many leaders, I believe that the black community is under attack, and that many of the community-based programs in our neighborhoods are insufficient for countering the rate at which that assault is taking place. No doubt, discrimination, racism, and the changing tide of political attitudes have combined to create a conservative cynicism that bulks at the thought of redressing America's unfair treatment of blacks. But unlike many of my colleagues, I differ on one important point. I do not believe that our biggest enemy is housed on Capitol Hill or in the legislature of Wisconsin. Rather, I contend that our most dangerous enemy has taken up the fight where many of us are too blind to see him, thus we continue to wage a losing battle against people and systems that are merely an outgrowth of our own inability to recognize the truth.

In his letter to the Ephesians Apostle Paul wrote: "For we do not wrestle against flesh and blood, but against principalities, against powers, against the rulers of the darkness of this age, against spiritual *hosts* of wickedness in heavenly *places*" (Ephesians 6:12, NKJV).

The enemy is not male or female, black or white, rich or poor. But according to Ephesians 6:12 the enemy is a spirit or a host of spirits organized into armed camps, operating from behind embattlements that are cloaked in secrecy (darkness) and upheld by power. Satan is that enemy!

Racism and discrimination are deplorable systems of destruction that have no place in a civilized society, and the men and women that continue to fuel these systems of evil are nothing less than wicked. But we have fought against these enemies for so long that we have been dirtied in the fight, and can scarcely recognize the enemy from ourselves. That is why in most of the major cities across America young black men and women are dying at the hands of their own at a rate greater than the mortality rate of the Iraqi war. For we continue to fight unsuccessfully against people who are merely the channels through which the real enemy operates.

Dr. Evans says, "Satan has been successful in getting us to fight people rather than fighting that which is causing people to be the way they are" (Evans, 1998, p.19). We spend enormous amounts of energy trying to change people, instead of trying to change the *condition* that is operating through them. Whenever Jesus Christ encountered a man or woman possessed with demons he never addressed himself to the person, but directed his attention to the demons that had taken possession of the person. Jesus knew, what we must ultimately understand, that Satan is the prince of this world (John 14:30), and the "spirit at work in the hearts of those who refuse to obey God" (Ephesians 2:2, NLT).

The wickedness we are witnessing on the battlegrounds of our cities is not the result of some human conspiracy, hatched in the clandestine boardrooms of America's riches' five percent. It is the calculated attack of spiritual forces that are running out of time, and are feverishly working through human agents to frustrate God's plan to save mankind.

The real battle will not be fought with weapons of steel but with weapons "...mighty in God for the pulling down of strongholds" (2 Corinthians 10:4, NKJV). If we are to win our children back we must begin to wage war against ourselves, because the real battle takes place within the broken down walls of our own communities. So goes the charge that comes down to us from the Apostle Paul, when he says, "Examine yourselves as to whether you are in the faith. Test yourselves. Do you not know yourselves, that Christ is in you? — unless indeed you are disqualified" (2 Corinthians 13:5, NKJV).

The Church is the last vestige of hope for a people who have lost their way wandering in a strange land. A people that have tasted the fruit of a tree called America and have all but abandoned God. Many of our leaders are not fit to lead us and have surrendered us to every kind of false god imaginable, while they strike deals with the devil to sacrifice our children at the alter of material expediency. I am reminded of the children of Israel in Elijah's day, when the leaders of that nation had misled the people with foreign values and strange gods (1 Kings 18:15-16). But I am also encouraged, for God always appears with a bright light of hope to draw his children back home (1 Kings 18:38-39). "For *there is* one God, and one mediator between God and men, the man Christ Jesus" (1 Timothy 2:5, KJV).

Jesus Christ is the Head of the Church! He is the Wheel in the middle of the Wheel. He is the Truth, the Way, and the Light. He is our Kindred Redeemer. He is the Lion of Judah. He is the Prince of Peace. He is the Savior of the world. He is the Son of God! He is the Bridge over which we must pass if we are to save our people.

Now that we understand the black community is under attack, and who the enemy actually is, let us take a look at the true nature of the circumstances that have allowed the adversary to make inroads into our community.

What Went Wrong

The book of Proverbs forms what I believe is a commentary on many black children in the enclaves of America. It reads: "The eye that mocks a father and scorns to obey a mother, the ravens of the valley will pick it out, and young vultures will devour it" (Proverbs 30:17, Amp.). Likewise, Proverbs 20:20 reads: "Whosoever curses his father or his mother, his lamp shall be put out in complete darkness."

When children in a society begin to challenge the wisdom of their elders, with malicious disregard and disrespect, then they make themselves a conduit for satanic forces to enter in a take control of them. They become easy prey for gangs, drug dealers, and hustlers that lay in ambush on every corner of our communities. These wayward youth go about trying to fill voids that have been created by their own disobedience. Their eyes have been drawn to things that go beyond their maturity to understand, and while unnatural desires are aroused in them, neighborhood vultures swoop in to confuse their senses. Finally they are left alone, alienated from themselves and the parents that bore them, until they are lost and turned out of sound understanding and blind as the day they were born. James said: "But each one is tempted when he is drawn away by his own desire and enticed. Then, when desire has conceived, it gives birth to sin; and sin, when it is full-grown, brings forth death" (James 1:14-15, NKJV).

It is critically important that we understand the forces that are at work in the lives of our children. First, we must realize that our children are under spiritual attack by an avowed enemy of God — Satan. The Apostle Peter has warned us to "Be careful! Watch out for attacks from the Devil, your great enemy. He prowls around like a roaring lion, looking for some victim to devour" (1 Peter 5:8, NLT). The very fact that the devil has to *find* someone to devour is an indication that he is not always successful. There are people that he is unsuccessful at devouring or destroying. Who are these people? They are people that are not so terrified by the "roar" of the lion that they forget what they are suppose to do when confronted by him. The Apostle James gives us the answer when he says, "So humble yourselves before God. Resist the Devil, and he will flee from you" (James 4:7, NLT).

The problem with many of us is that we are like the deer, which has halted before the stream to quench its thirst, defenselessly lapping its fill, when all of a sudden from the nearby brush comes the roar of the lion! The deer becomes petrified and unable to move, long enough to see the beast leap from the brush, and in a fit of fear it leaps in the opposite direction, only to find itself between the jaws of another beast it could have outrun on its worst day.

We need to acknowledge that there is a "moral" problem that forms the basis for many of the problems in our community. We cannot ignore the misplaced values of a generation of people that have been reared in homes decimated by drugs, alcohol, sexual abuse, verbal abuse, and a host of other domestic abnormalities. In short, we are giving way to a generation of youth that have turned away in disgust as we praise God on Sunday mornings after having drunk ourselves silly at the club the night before. Thus, they can find no lasting value in a life spent believing in a god who is purported to be able to do all things, and yet witness daily the defeat gleaned in their parents' eyes as they *struggle* to trust in God.

The Church must be watchful and always on guard against the prospect of allowing the pressures of this world to lull it into accepting things into the body of Christ that are opposed to the Gospel of God. Our leaders must strive to live "blameless" before the throne of grace (1 Timothy 3:2, NKJV), and exhort the believers to live "…holy, acceptable to God…" (Romans 12:1, NKJV), which is the least that God expects of us. They must be men and women of integrity "…not like those hucksters — and there are many of them — who preach just for money" (2 Corinthians 2:17, NLT).

The sad truth is that, while we have many great ministries in communities across the United States, many of the scandals that have rocked the modern church have helped to weaken the reputation of the Church, and has stolen the thunder from God. These scandals have become a stumbling block to lost souls, searching for a safe harbor to lay down anchor, and have crippled the church in its efforts to offer solutions to the moral dilemma now facing our people. If the African American community is to combat the problems that has infected it like a virus, then the church must begin to live by the creed it preaches, rather than cowering beneath the weight of a world that demands allegiance to its gods. "And do not be conformed to this world, but be transformed by the renewing of your mind, that you may prove what is that good and acceptable and perfect will of God" (Romans 12:2, NKJV).

In *When God Comes To Church*, Ortlund (2000) summed up the whole of the affair when he said, "Men have forgotten God; that's why all this has happened" (p.173). He goes on to say, "We've tried to reinvent church to attract the entertainment-addicted public and we're left with not much of a message to that public. We've tried signs and wonders, self-esteem and emotional healing, health and wealth... and still the church languishes in mediocrity and still the world potters on its way to hell" (Ortlund, 2000, pp.174-75). But in the final analysis it will not be our ingenuity and well-meaning promotions that will win souls to Christ— God himself "mediated to us by his Spirit and declared from his Word — he is the power and attraction and genius of the church" (Ortlund, 2000, pp.173-74).

We are in a life and death struggle to save a generation of people who are privy to information they are too immature to process. Just the other day I was looking around the community center where I work, and I noticed a valentine greeting that one of the fourth grade girls had written and taped to the wall. It read: "Roses are red, violets are blue, your man is over there cheating on you." My question to the reader is what does a girl in the fourth grade do with that kind of information? Where does she learn it? Why does she know it?

It is time that black leaders realign themselves with the realities that now face us. We can no longer bury our heads in the sand while our communities are under siege by the very people we continue to defend. But "*Let* love *be* without hypocrisy. Abhor what is evil. Cling to what is good" (Romans 12:9, NKJV), and "Do not be overcome by evil, but overcome evil with good" (Romans 12:21, NKJV).

Our children are under ceaseless attacks by an enemy that neither sleeps nor tires of the fight, and lays in wait while their restless souls reach beyond themselves for answers. The Church must be vigilant, striving always to be the moral compass for communities struggling against the tide of changing fortunes, and quick to respond to foreign enemies that attempt to infect the believers with ideas better left to the world. We must go back to the old landmark and "earnestly contend for the faith which was once for all delivered to the saints" (Jude 1: 3,

NKJV). We must go back to the blood of a dying savior torn and ripped at the cross — victorious over the sting of death that was swallowed up by his resurrection (1 Corinthians 15:55-56). We must, without compromise or consideration for who we might offend, give to the world our only solution for sin: "Jesus Christ and Him crucified" (1 Corinthians 2:2, KJV), "For *there is* one God, and one mediator between God and men, the man Christ Jesus" (1 Timothy 2:5, KJV).

It is precisely at the point of *mediation* (Christ Jesus) that we either succeed in our efforts or fail in our understanding of what is ultimately at stake in our communities. For the truth is that we are so busy fighting against people and systems that we neglect to take the battle into the camp of the real enemy. That negligence rarely leads to any serious examination of ourselves, and usually lulls us into a complacency that allows us to blame others while watching, as the conditions in our communities grow worse.

3 > Jesus Bridged The Gap

For *there is* one God, and one mediator
between God and men, the man Christ Jesus.

1 Timothy 2:5 (KJV)

The nature of what is going wrong in
our communities is an outgrowth of an inward
condition that has gone untreated far too long. It is
the absence of a dependable bridge across the abyss
of our spiritual dilemma that prevents our approach
to God, and manifests itself in the wretchedness
we witness daily in lives of a people that have all
but lost their way. But we have seen these people
before, over 2,500 years ago as recorded in the book
of 1 Kings. They were the children of Israel, who
had received the promises God; the deliverance of
God; the measure of God's favor, but instead of
honoring God for the abundance of his glory they
turned away to other *gods*. But while they satisfied

their hunger for perverse and forbidden pleasures, God interrupted their lives with a demonstration so powerful it has outlasted the crumbled remains of their time. For our God is a jealous god and will not share his glory with anyone or any thing (Isaiah 48:11).

1 Kings 18:19-40, while specific to the historical circumstances of the Jews, forms the backdrop for what I believe we are witnessing in our nation today, especially as it relates to African Americans. Those historical accounts are the powerful demonstration of a God who will step down into time, consume us with his miraculous feats, and overwhelm us with his all-encompassing mercy. But first he must draw us away from our preoccupation with the gods of this world, so that he can open to us the door of his forgiveness and the windows of his blessings.

God opened such a window to me one day in December 2002 during a consecration. I was reading the book of 1 Kings 18, when some where from a place inside God revealed to me such truths that it blew my mind! He brought home to me the nature of the human condition and the struggle that rages within us to find a balance between good and evil. It was from the seeds of that revelation that God birthed in me *Bridge Over Troubled Waters.* But before I get ahead myself, lets take a journey back over the pages of time, and unravel the twisted tale of a people quite like us.

The Children of Israel had been divided into two Kingdoms: Israel, in the north, and Judah, in the south. For the remainder of this chapter we will focus on the Northern Kingdom of Israel.

The legacy of Israel's sins had given birth to seven kings who had turned the heart of the people away from the true worship of God. The rulers had dispensed with the priests that God had anointed, and replaced them with men-for-hire, who served the cause of man instead serving in the will of God. They ruled from Shechem, Tirza, and Samaria in honor of foreign gods that lacked any power or ability to raise the moral condition of the people. But Ahab, the seventh king of Israel, "did evil in the sight of the Lord, more than all who *were* before him" (1 Kings 16:30, NKJV). He finished the work of his father, Omri, who had begun the construction of a city on a hill, called Samaria (1 Kings 16:24). There he erected an altar for the *storm god,* Baal, in a house dedicated to Baal's worship, and for his wife, Jezebel, he made an Asherah, a wood goddess (1 Kings 16:32-33).

The Prophet Elijah exploded unto the pages of history in 875 BC, when the kingdom of Israel was in its infancy as a divided kingdom. He appeared before King Ahab and announced: "As the Lord

God of Israel lives, before whom I stand, there shall not be dew nor rain these years, except at my word" (1 Kings 17:1, NKJV).

This is the first glimpse that scripture offers us of Elijah, the Prophet from Tishbe. A man clothed in camel's hair, modest in appearance, and everything that luxury and extravagance was not. His only defense — the Lord God that lives! This man steps out of the obscurity of the desert, exposes himself to danger, in order to challenge a king that had been so bold as to defy God. But in the face of imminent danger this man, without an army, without weapons of mass destruction, without royal papers of introduction, confronts the sins of a king with the authority of a God that lives!

This first meeting between Elijah and Ahab marked the beginning of a struggle that was soon to contrast the power of the living God with the impotence of a dying world. For you can be sure that wherever God has established the Spirit of truth the enemy has established a stronghold by which to attack what God has ordained. God says, "You shall have no other gods before me" (Exodus 20:3, NKJV). Satan says, "…fall down and worship me" (Mathew 4:9, NKJV). God says, "seek first the kingdom" (Mathew 6:33a, NKJV). Satan says, "All these things I will give to you…" (Mathew 4:9, NKJV). While God establishes laws that will bring us into "the promise of life which is in Christ Jesus" (2 Timothy 1:1, NKJV), Satan sets up strongholds of illusion to "...steal, and to kill, and to destroy" (John 10:10, NKJV) what God is trying to manifest in our lives.

If we understood what was really at stake in the battle and skirmishes that were ripping our communities apart — the living God versus a dying world — then we would begin to appreciate the healing power of God's love as he confronts the dead situations in our lives. It is when we have come face to face with the rebellion of our youth, rampant crime rates, escalating teenage pregnancies, abortion, and countless social ills that Elijah steps forward and demonstrates for all time the solution for attacking these problems.

First, we must gain a greater appreciation for the power that is necessary to generate change in our social and personal situations. That is why Elijah declares, "As the Lord God of Israel lives, before whom I stand" (1 Kings 17:1a, NKJV). To effect meaningful change, in a community that has been ravaged by various anti-social elements, it is necessary to be plugged into an energy source with the power to generate that change.

Second, we must be bold enough to confront the condition that is standing in the way of change. Even though that condition appears to be as gigantic as the mountain upon which King Ahab has built his city. We must be willing to surrender ourselves to a powerful and mighty God that wages war against "…every high thing that exalts itself against the knowledge of God" (2 Corinthians 10:5a, NKJV).

Third, we must learn to speak the word of truth to that condition, "bringing every thought into captivity to the obedience of Christ" (2 Corinthians 10:5b, NKJV). We must declare, "there shall not be dew nor rain these years, except at my word" (1 Kings 17:1b, NKJV). For until we stop nourishing and feeding the appetite of our lusts we cannot begin the process of drying up the decayed and diseased conditions that eat at the heart of our communities. In short, the only way to deal with a sin that persists in our lives is to dry up the conditions that allow it to grow stronger. Elijah called this sibling-sin, dew (Psalms 110:3b), or the resulting manifestation of missing the mark on a continual bases. He was speaking to the negative conditions that were responsible for the continued proliferation of sin (rain). He was intimating the fact that "when desire has conceived, it gives birth to sin; and sin, when it is full-grown, brings forth death" (James 1:15, NKJV). In a sense, the rain is the mother of sin (in its conception), while dew is the sibling of sin (as it grows out of control).

I believe that much of the problem in dealing with sin in our lives comes from the way we perceive sin. I'm not sure if the average believer truly understands that the nature of all sin is demonic, and therefor derives from Satan. Sin is more than merely *missing* the mark. It is a manifestation of a demonic barrier that is sent (from Satan) to block or hinder our relationship with God. The bible often speaks about sin in terms of the "desires of the flesh" or "godless human nature" (Galatians 5:17, Amp.). Those desires are said to be in a continual *battle* with the Spirit, giving birth to such things as loose living, wrong thinking, unashamed boldness, material worship, drug addiction, hostility, quarreling, jealousy, rage, selfishness, gang activity, prejudice, envy, drunkenness, and wild partying (Galatians 5: 19-21).

Symbolically, in 1 King 17:1, God shut up the sky as a sign that it had become necessary to cut off the people from the spiritual spring that was bringing them life. For in the midst of His nourishing them they had allowed the impostor of rain, Baal, to flourish in their lives. Thus as proof of his authenticity God withdrew himself from Israel, and allowed them to be blinded by their self-imposed wills.

Baal and **Asherah** represent the reality of worldly treasures that have captured our imaginations and passions. Baal is the false hope that deceives us into relying on created things that have no real power to change the condition of our lives. Asherah is the distorted result of false hopes that have given birth to all manner of sin.

God is not "slack concerning *His* promise, as some count slackness, but longsuffering toward us, not willing that any should perish but that all should come unto repentance" (2 Peter 3:9, NKJV). While it is true that the Lord may allow our false hopes and distorted reliance to fail us, he is still actively pursuing our ultimate salvation. And just when we are about to lose faith over our situations God again sends Elijah to turn our hearts back to him. Once He has succeeded in drawing us away from the gods of this world, then he opens to us the door of transformation and the window of His renewing (Romans 12:2).

After a period of fasting, praying, and relying on the nourishment of God man and woman returns to the scene where the Lord reveals the mystery that will release them from the chains that hold them. He knows they are ready, because he has stopped up the sky, stolen the dew, and held back the clouds from rain. Now the storm god Baal has lost his hold, for in these three and a half years there has been no rain, and that impostor, Asherah, goddess of wood, has been unable to flourish for lack of the dew.

Make Up Your Mind

God comes once more to challenge the condition that still holds us prisoner, and says, "Send and gather all of Israel to me on Mount Carmel, the four hundred and fifty prophets of Baal, and the four hundred prophets of Asherah, who eat at Jezebel's table" (1 Kings 18:19, NKJV). In other words, the Lord is calling us out in the heat of our rebellion, in the midst of our wrongdoing — to meet Him at the place where we have planted all our hopes and fed all our passions — on Mount Carmel! In America! In our Communities! In our Homes! In our Lives!

Ahab called together all the children of Israel and the prophets to the meeting place where God would challenge the hearts of a wayward nation. But more importantly, it was here that Elijah underscored the principle of individual accountability, when he asked the people: "How long will you falter between two opinions? If the Lord is God, follow Him; but if Baal, follow him" (1 K. 18:21, NKJV).

The principle of individual responsibility precludes the cry of a people who say, "'The fathers have eaten sour grapes, And the children's teeth are set on edge'" (Jeremiah 31:29, NKJV). Each of us, barring any mental defect, is endowed with the rational ability to choose right from wrong. According to the Apostle Paul all of us demonstrate that "…the essential requirements of the law are written…" in our "…hearts and are operating there…" wherein our "…consciences (sense of right and wrong) also bear witness…"(Romans 2:15, Amp.). Thus, even while the king and the godless values of society exert some degree of pressure on us to turn from the true worship of God — Elijah draws attention to the fact that each of us still has a personal responsibility to *choose* between good and evil.

Again, I believe that the black community is under attack, and that many of the secular programs developed to effect meaningful change (in our communities) are not enough for countering the rate at which the assault is taking place. Discrimination, racism, and the changing tide of political attitudes have combined to continue America's unfair treatment of blacks. But we can not hope to successfully combat those social and political ills until we first summon our people to Mount Carmel, along with all their worldly distractions and failed hopes. There we must speak to the condition of their individual hearts: *how long will you be crippled by your inability to understand that God is real, and that lasting success will be but a faint whisper until you make a decision to live wholly for God.*

But we can not live wholly for God, divorced from our selfish desires, until we understand our individual wretchedness apart from God. That is why the Apostle Paul cried, "O wretched man that I am! Who will deliver me from this body of death?" (Romans 7:24, NKJV). In other words, what will be able to save me from the practices of the flesh (Galatians 5:19)?

Naked Before God

While our hearts are thrown open before God' s piercing stare we answer not a word (1 Kings 18:21), because of the awesome weight of our uncleanness before the presence of God. For all of us in our inmost parts know that we are unworthy of God's tender mercies, and in the moment of our awareness (that we have served other things in place of God) we are left naked and ashamed as first our parents were in the Garden of Eden. But it is only in our nakedness that we are vulnerable to the truth, and the Lord can step in and expose the forces of evil that seem to outnumber the good (1 Kings 18:22). In that moment of vulnerability the Lord lays down the challenge to us:

"Let two bulls be given us; let them choose one bull for themselves and cut it in pieces and lay it on the wood but put no fire to it. I will dress the other bull, lay it on the wood, and put no fire to it. Then you call on the name of your god, and I will call on the name of the Lord; and the *One* who answers by fire, let Him be God" (1 Kings 18:23-24, NKJV).

The stage was now set; the nature of good and evil had been given equal opportunities within the realm of possibility, and the people had opened themselves to the reality of a God who would not be outdone by substitutes. But before the Lord of *fire* could ignite the embers of the peoples' souls he had to allow them to be tried by the old deceptions that still clung to them.

Saints, you must understand that before the Lord can release you from the sins that weigh you down he may have to permit Satan to have some rule over your flesh. But do not get discouraged, but learn to "count it all joy when you fall into various trials, knowing that the testing of your faith produces patience. But let patience have its perfect work, that you may be perfect and complete, lacking nothing " (James 1:2-4, NKJV).

But after the prophets of Baal have prepared their sacrifice, leaped and danced in feverish desperation about the altar, and cried in wild expectation to their god from morning until noon, evening fast approaches when the Lord of Hosts is ready to appear (1 Kings 18:26-29). For there has been "no voice, no answer, no one who paid attention" (1 Kings 18:29, NKJV), only the sickening smell of running blood as it gushed from the wounds of false prophets, that had loss their hold over the lives of the saints (1 Kings 18:28).

When we take a closer look at the frenzied and almost psychotic behavior of the prophets of Baal we are struck by an inescapable truth: the flesh always struggles to maintain control of our hearts. The Apostle Paul observed as much when he said:

"The desires of the flesh are opposed to the [Holy] Spirit, and the [desires of the] Spirit are opposed to the flesh (godless human nature); for these are antagonistic to each other [continually withstanding and in conflict with each other], so that you are not free but are prevented from doing what you desire to do" (Galatians 5:17, Amp.).

It is important to note that in our Christian walk we are coming up against some powerful desires that act in ways that often makes no sense. We often find ourselves in extramarital relationships, which while destructive, seem to hold for us some perverse sense of pleasure. By the same token, we are often slaves to habits and addictions that control us so intensely that even while our lives lie before us in ruins, we are powerless to stop those obsessions: drugs, sex, gambling, pornography, rape, murder, and all manner of compulsive disorders. But when at long last the fasting has ended, the prayers have ceased, and the sun has inched its way back into the waiting hands of twilight — hope is renewed

— Elijah steps forth again with a final plea to the people, "Come near me" (1 Kings 18:30, NKJV). In short, since God has loosened the chains of your deception, allow him to deliver you from the lusts that keep you prisoner. Allow him to *repair* your diseased heart, the altar that has been torn down by Jezebel; the queen that sits in wait for spiritual midgets whose passions have been perverted by sin. Draw near to the Lord with a willingness that ushers you into his presence in worship, and floods your heart with expectation at the mere thought of his returning grace. Like David say, "Create in me a clean heart, O God; and renew a right spirit within me" (Psalms 51:10, KJV). Now you are ready to receive the Spirit from heaven needed to liberate your heart from all semblance of wickedness. "Now the Lord is the Spirit; and where the Spirit of the Lord *is*, there *is* liberty" (2 Corinthians 3:17, NKJV).

Getting Back To God

Elijah takes seven basic steps to liberate the Israelites from the worship of Baal. One, he rebuilds the old altar of the true God that had been broken down by Jezebel (1 Kings 18:30). Two, he takes 12 stones, according to the number of the sons of Jacob, "to whom the word of the Lord came, saying, Israel shall be your name" (1 Kings 18:31, Amp.), and built an altar (1 Kings 18:32). Three, he dug a trench three feet wide around the altar (1 Kings 18:32). Four, he "put the wood in order and cut the bull in pieces and laid it on the wood" (1 Kings 18:33, Amp.). Five, he had the people fill 4 jars three times, and pour it over the offering (1 Kings 18:33-35). Six, at the time of the evening offering of sacrifice Elijah prayed to the Lord, calling to remembrance His connection to the Children of Israel, and asking that He demonstrate His sovereign power, and thereby justify His Word and turn the heart of the people (1 Kings 18:36-37). Immediately the "fire of the Lord fell and consumed the burnt sacrifice and the wood and the stones and the dust, and also licked up the water that was in the trench" (1 Kings 18:38, NKJV). The people seeing it, fell to the ground in praise, saying, "The Lord, He is God! The Lord, He is God!" (1Kings 18:39, NKJV).

Seven, Elijah instructed the people to seize the prophets of Baal. "They seized them, and Elijah brought them to the brook of Kishon, and [as God's law required] slew them there" (1 Kings 18:40, Amp.).

I believe that the events in 1 Kings 18:19-40 is a graphic demonstration of God's awesome power and all encompassing mercy. But more than that, these events hold the key to addressing what is wrong in our communities.

The nature of what is going wrong in our communities is an outgrowth of an inward condition that has gone untreated far too long. It is the absence of a **dependable bridge** across the **trench** of our sins that hampers our approach to God.

Elijah offers us a unique perspective on how to deal with that inward condition (of sin) that separates us from God. Thus, there are seven basic steps that are indispensable for liberating our communities from the rate of decline we are now witnessing.

Step One: Christian leaders must "contend earnestly for the faith which was once for all delivered to the saints" (Jude 1:3, NKJV). Our churches must once again become bastions of hope for people lost in the maze of a dying world. We must be less driven by the impulse to use modern-day gimmicks to attract the "entertainment-addicted public" (Ortlund, 2000, pp.174-75), and more driven to preach "Jesus Christ and Him crucified" (1 Corinthians 2:2, NKJV) as "the power and attraction and genius of the church" (Ortlund, 2000, pp.173-74). Thus, our "faith should not be in the wisdom of men but in the power of God" (1 Corinthians 2:5, NKJV). This contemporary appeal to the Church is what the elders called going back to the old landmark, and why Elijah "repaired the [old] altar of the Lord" that had been *broken down* through custom and secular allegiance (1 Kings 18:30, Amp.).

Step Two: We must rear our children in the fear of God, and train them "in the way" they "should go" and when they are old, they "will not depart from it" (Proverbs 22:6b, NKJV).

We must change the focus of our efforts into the community to be sure that they are based on the biblical principles of the Gospel. Otherwise, we will have wasted our energies trying to raise Jacob instead of developing the necessary circumstances that bring forth the character of Israel.

Step Three: We need to understand that at the core of every human striving is a gulf (sin) that separates us from God. It is the void at the heart of every striving; the pulse in ancient philosophy that first prompted the question, "Who am I?" It is the veil that prevents our personal relationship with God (Numbers 3:26), and keeps us at arms length from the glory of God's righteousness. Thus, it is when we are face to face with the irrational activities of our youth that we understand that they are still searching for a way to bridge the gap that keeps them from seeing the face of God (Exodus 33:11)!

Step Four: Understanding the nature at the heart of every striving now gives us insight into the method for bringing us back into fellowship with the Lord. We must admit our hopelessness apart from

God, and bring our sins to Him. But we must be careful to identify those sins and not merely assume that God will accept them as we daily present them in prayer, "God forgive me for *all* my sins."

Elijah put the "wood in order" and then he "cut the bull in pieces and laid it on the wood" (1 Kings 18:33, Amp.). He ordered the wood as a demonstration that the prophets who ate at Jezebel's table were fed from a source that had order and proceeded from an authority. Need I remind you that Satan is the authority from which every sin proceeds, and that his kingdom is ordered according to his evil plan (Ephesians 6:12). In order for the "Lord of Hosts" to conquer the ordered plan of Satan against your life, God needs you to single out the *pieces* that you need him to come against. In a sense, we need to redirect our aim, and stop blaming others for our problems, and accept individual responsibility for our shortcomings as a people.

Step Five: We must learn to operate in faith (Hebrews 11:1,6). Thus, step five is a pivotal stage in God's plan to save us from ourselves, because it marks the realization that God is able to do what is impossible for man. The laws of physics do not apply to Him, neither do our failed attempts at understanding Him through science. And while the 12 stones of the altar tie him to the Jews; the twelve times that water is poured over the altar ties

Him to the Gentiles. It looks to a time when people from every nation will stand "before the throne and before the Lamb, clothed with white robes, with palm branches in their hands" (Revelation 7: 9, NKJV).

So even while we may receive the promises of God, it is crucial that we do not neglect to work out our "own salvation with fear and trembling; for it is God who works in you both to will and to do for *His* good pleasure" (Philippians 2:12-13, NKJV). That is why the Apostle Paul was able to exclaim the affirmative response to God's calling when he said:

"Yes, and if I am being poured out *as a drink offering* on your sacrifice and service of your faith, I am glad and rejoice with you all" (Philippians 2:17, NKJV).

When we approach every situation in faith then our hearts are turned in expectation of God's wonders, and in the moment that we have presented our body as a "living sacrifice, holy, acceptable to God" (Romans 12:1, NKJV), he drenches us with His glory.

Step Six: We must appeal to the promises of God, and invoke His presence in the midst of our dilemmas. We must pray for God to send revival into our churches so that the heart of the people may be turned back to Him (1 Kings 18:37). Like

David we must ask, "Won't you revive us again, so your people can rejoice in you"(Psalms 85:6, NLT)? We must ask him to replace hearts fat like grease (Psalms 119:70), that have loss understanding of God (Romans 10:2), with hearts clean and renewed by the Spirit of Truth (John 16:13).

God does not seek long, repetitious prayers (Mathew 6:7), but prayers based on *faith* (Mathew 9:29) in a God that "gives life to the dead and calls those things which do not exist as though they did" (Romans 4:17, NKJV). Such was the prayer of Elijah, that appealed to who God is, "the God of Abraham, Isaac, and Israel" (1 Kings 18:36, NKJV), and what He is able to do: to change the heart of the people (1 Kings 18:37).

Clearly, we must appeal to the covenant relationship that God has established with us through the faith that has now been delivered unto us. Romans 10:9 (NKJV) sets out the terms of that covenant or contract when it says, "that if you confess with your mouth the Lord Jesus and believe in your heart that God has raised him from the dead, you will be saved." While this most simple remedy lies at the heart of all our troubles, it is perhaps most baffling to witness how many of us stumble over this truth. For the Apostle Peter, quoting the Prophet Isaiah said, "'The stone which builders rejected Has become the chief cornerstone, and A stone of stumbling And a rock of offense'" (1 Peter. 2: 7-8, NKJV).

Step Seven: When the conviction of the Lord (fire) consumes all of the sins in our hearts, and has "licked up the water that was in the trench" (1 Kings 18:38, NKJV), we are ready to have him "renew a right spirit within" us (Psalms 51:10, NLT).

The Lord's renewing is like a breath of fresh air, and all we can do in response to this *breathing* is praise Him for who He is (1 Kings 18:39). Clearly, this is none other than the Holy Spirit, which descends from above *like* fire, destroying the hold of sin over our lives (Acts 1:8, 2:2-3).

Finally, at this stage of completion, we must slay the false prophets at the brook of Kishon, or the place where *traps* are set (1 Kings 18:40). Here we must once and for all make a decision to live for God, and allow His enabling power to take hold of "every weight, and the sin which so easily ensnares us" (Hebrews 12:1, NKJV). Then, "the body of sin might be done away with, that we should no longer be slaves to sin" (Romans 6:6, NKJV).

I believe that the separation between God and man explains most if not all of the violence and crime plaguing our communities. It is the absence of a dependable bridge across the trench of our sins that hampers our approach to God. I was led to this conclusion when one thing more than anything else struck me about the account in 1 Kings 18:19-40: the *trench!* For even while God's power was manifest with such miraculous results, consuming the "burnt sacrifice and the wood and the stones and the dust, and also licked up the water that was in the trench" (1 Kings 18:38, Amp.), it left the trench in place. Why?

I believe that the answer is given to us in 1 Timothy 2:5 (KJV), when the Apostle Paul declares," *there is* one God, and one mediator between God and men, the man Christ Jesus." Jesus Christ is the bridge that gives us access to God, and frees us from the body of sin and confusion that lies at the heart of our existence.

The trench represents the lone souls of our wayward youth who have yet to embrace the truth about Jesus Christ, but have been trapped by all manner of secular lusts that have robbed their hearts of even a semblance of light. So now in every corner of America we have young men and women growing up opposed to the very source from which flows their only hope: **Christ Jesus, and him crucified!**

If our children are to be snatched from the waiting jaws of Satan, we must develop a strategy for winning them back, and in no small way, I have attempted to outline a method of attack based on some insights gleaned from the pages of our sacred text.

A final word and warning comes down to us from the time of Hosea, when the people misdiagnosed their symptoms as a political problem owing to outside forces, instead of a moral problem owing to an internal condition. Ortlund (2000) spelled it out quite nicely when he said:

"We can see our symptoms easily enough but we do not diagnose the disease wisely. And so we apply irrelevant, ineffective remedies. And we risk antagonizing God even further by treating *him* as if he were irrelevant. How dimly we grasp the true relevance of spiritual things for living real life in this tough world" (p. 68).

4 > When Boys Become Men

Then Jacob was left alone; and a Man
wrestled with him until the breaking of day.

Genesis 32:24 (Amp.)

The rituals and rites that mark the passage
from childhood to adulthood have varied from
century to century and from culture to culture.
And while there is no one cultural rite of passage
that is the best fit for every people; the scriptures
provides us with some practical points that help us
to understand the various stages that help shape the
life of people.

Before we look at the process of spiritual
growth as outlined in scripture, it is necessary
to define what the rite of passage is. The **rite of
passage** is "a ceremony in some cultures marking
the passing to another, more advanced stage, as to
puberty or adulthood" (Webster's, 1986).

The Hebrew term *Bar Mitzvah,* literally means *man of duty*, a term applied to all male Jews attaining the age of thirteen. This is a period usually marked by a ceremony that extended "to the boy the adult privilege of reading the Torah, or being called to Torah, the first Sabbath after his thirteenth birthday" (Birnbaum, 1964, p. 94). This was possibly the most important period in the life of a Jewish male, for according to custom it was a period when all religious rights pertained to him. But more importantly, it marked the period when it was believed that the male child was able to discern right from wrong.

This chapter will provide us with a biblical view for understanding the rite of passage as a period of spiritual maturity in the life of a person, marked by various stages of development. But more than that, it will provide us with an explanation for understanding what happens when the rite of passage or spiritual maturity is absent in the lives of *boys who become men.*

I believe that a large number of youth caught up in the criminal justice system of our nation are a by-product of scared little children who never took the rite of passage. They are boys bound for manhood without the adequate training or tools to operate within the social arena of life. They are the wounded and fragile men who move from one sexual exploit to the next, attempting to validate their manhood by the number of women they are able to bed. They are the alcoholics and drug addicted men who have passed from adolescence to obsolescence in their attempts to escape responsibility for their lives. They are the thirty-to-forty year old *boys* who have spent the greater part of their lives living at the apron strings of their mothers. They are the little boys who never quite grew up, and kept looking for a mother in every woman they met. They are the boys who had children who had children by other children that never became men. They are the result of what happens when we fail to nurture them through the rites of passage from boyhood to manhood.

I remember receiving a call from a good friend of mine, and she was concerned about her son, who was now seventeen, and was attempting to put back together the scattered pieces of his life. He was back in school trying to regain some semblance of the good grades he had received up until his freshman year in high school. He had experimented with alcohol and marijuana, and now he was hundreds of miles form his mother, staying with an aunt, struggling desperately to change his life. But in his struggle to reconcile himself to change he was dealing with the realities of peer pressure, and the still small voice of the Holy Spirit prompting him to stay the course.

I realized by speaking to his mother what was going on, because I had been there before, and no one was there to guide me through. So I called him and listened to him, and began to see me at seventeen all over again. He was scared, confused, hurt, insecure and unsure about how he fit into life. He was experiencing feelings and thoughts he could not explain, and hanging out with people who were not matched to his strivings in life. He felt different, out of place and out of mind he was forced to wrestle with himself and the decisions confronting him daily. In short, he was reaching out for someone that would guide him through the rite of passage, "until the breaking of day" (Genesis 32:24, KJV).

I let him know that what he was feeling was normal for a young man, and that the feeling of being outside the peer group was a result of God trying to wrest him from circumstances that were harmful to him. I explained to him that he was experiencing feelings that came from the special anointing God had placed on his life. And no matter how hard he tried he would always find himself around people, whose lack of knowledge would make him feel different, because he was. The last I heard he was doing well in school and even had a job.

Father, I pray that the words that are impressed upon the space of these pages are a true reflection of your power being released at my hand. And that whatever hand is guided to turn these pages and that whatever eyes take in these words may find solace in discovery and healing in these truths. Amen.

When we look at the life of a human being what we see is three distinct stages of human development: childhood, adolescence, and adulthood. Each stage is marked by very specific physical and mental changes that tend to separate one stage from the other. For example, childhood seems to be marked by rapid and constant changes in the physical body as well as increased perceptiveness in the mental capabilities of the child. Adolescence seems to be a shift from childhood to a *middle* period where various biological changes tend to impact on the emotional aspects of the (once) child, and usually asserts itself in a stage of rebellion against traditional family structures. Finally, adulthood marks a period where independence and added responsibility are expected to assert themselves, and the higher functions of the brain are suppose to be at their height.

Growing In God

I believe that God has revealed in scripture the keys for understanding what is necessary for successful passage from one stage of human development to the next. Thus, in Genesis 32:24, what we have is a ceremonial rite of passage from where we're coming from to where we're going. In the final analysis, each passage must be marked by a *move* from God.

In order to be stable in adulthood we must be assured in adolescence that the direction of our life is based on something beyond our immediate circumstances. On that wise, the child must know that when he cries there is someone near to care for his needs. He must know that immediate needs are met by future expectations.

Genesis 32:24 reads, "Then Jacob was left alone; and a Man wrestled with him until the breaking of day." This passage points to three distinct stages in human development: (1) being left alone with God (2) struggling with God, and (3) breaking free from fear. Thus, at each successive stage in life, God is moving us to a place where He can deal with us alone. The importance of "aloneness" cannot be underscored enough, because it is precisely in the hour of our separation from outside distractions that the Lord is able to come in and deal with us.

The two Hebrew terms used to describe the condition of Jacob are *yâthar*, "to remain after," and *bad*, "alone or apart (from)." The general idea is that Jacob had reached a point in his life when his past deceitfulness (yâthar) had to be separated (bad) from his present yearning to embrace the bigger challenges waiting to confront him in the future. Jacob remained trapped by the issues of a past that had sent him like a fugitive from the comfort of his father's house to the refuge of his uncle's house. Like many of us, Jacob was trying to understand who he *is* as opposed to who he had come to believe he was.

To some degree, Jacob represents a time in life when all of us see ourselves through the murky and dust-covered mirror of life. It is a time when we are attempting to define who we are amid the changing seasons of time. Like Jacob, we are often perplexed by the struggle inside to separate the "who" we are from the "who" we were.

I believe that the reality of who we *are* as opposed to who we *were* awaits a providential move of God, who must release light into our souls, in order for our true selves to emerge from beneath the murky depths of sin. The Apostle Paul made reference to this in 1Corinthians 13:12 (Amp.) when he said:

"For now we are looking in a mirror that gives only a dim (blurred) reflection [of reality as in a riddle or enigma], but then [when perfection comes] we shall see in reality *and* face to face!"

In cities across America young black boys and girls are struggling to come to terms with a crisis in their identity. The Jacobs of America are desperately scratching against the mirrors of their lives trying to catch a glimpse of themselves as they pass through life on their way to uncertainty. We are now faced with the task of coming to grips with that reality, and forming strategies for addressing it.

Much of who we are is based on where we come from, and the circumstances that have colored us on the canvass of life. It is no accident that almost every physiological and psychological questionnaire seeks to find out specific information about our family history. For it is no secret that certain physical and mental conditions are directly or indirectly tied to who our parents were. So that any honest portrayal of truth must look back to a time when all of us were but the clay upon which life left its impression.

If we take a look at the family tree of Jacob, through his father Isaac and his grandfather Abraham, we are struck by a reoccurring theme in the life of three women who stand at the center of world history: Sarah, Rebekah, and Rachel. THEY WERE BARREN!

The Hebrew term 'âqâr means, "failing to produce offspring," and is derived from the root word 'qar, meaning, "to pluck up." This term says as much about the physical condition of those women as it does about the psychological condition of their children. Upon closer examination we see that the conditions that form the early childhood experiences of Jacob speak volumes about the childhood traumas that lead to sibling rivalries, displacement, and eventually family crises.

Perhaps the first sign that there would be trouble in Jacob's family came at a time of great joy in the life of Isaac and his wife, Rebekah. When, after 20 years of waiting and praying, the Lord opened the womb of Rebekah and brought forth a double blessing in the birth of two sons (Genesis 25: 21). But beneath the surface of this long awaited blessing lie the seeds of discontent and trickery that would eventually become the spawning bed of hatred that would split the family in two. In Genesis 25: 22-23 (Amp.) we read:

"[Two] children struggled together within her; and she said, If it is so [that the Lord has heard our prayer], why am I like this? And she went to inquire of the Lord. The Lord said to her, [The founder of] two nations are in your womb, and the separation of two peoples has begun in your body; the one people shall be stronger than the other, and the elder shall serve the younger."

I believe that within the context of Jacob's experience at the brook of Jabbok (Genesis 32:23-24), he is a *struggling to break free* from a past that had marked his tutelage under his mother. He is struggling to somehow find a way to come to terms with the mistakes that drove his brother to say some twenty years earlier, "Is not he rightly named Jacob? For he has supplanted me these two times. He took away my birthright, and now look, he has taken away my blessing" (Genesis 27:36, NKJV)!

At The Crossroads

Jacob had come to the crossroads of life, when he needed to go back home, where he was forced to run from his brother who had sworn that upon the death of his father, Isaac, he would kill him (Genesis 27: 41-42). Barren, empty, and alone Jacob was at a place where everyone must go when they can no longer stay where they are, and they can scarce move forward without putting to rest their past. For the past is like an enormous weight strapped to your back, slowing your progress as you lumber forward to take hold of the things before you.

In the Genesis account we see a picture of Jacob loaded down by the crippling effects of fear, remorse, guilt, and shame as he labors to move in the direction God has directed him. But even while the storms of life raged around him God frequently appeared to reassure him that he was moving in the right direction. Thus, we read, "Jacob went on his way, and God's angels met him. When Jacob saw them, he said, This is God's army! So he named that place Mahannaim [two armies]" (Genesis 32:1-2, Amp.).

When the Lord prompts you to leave the comfort of what you have come to know, He will always send you the support you need to meet the tasks ahead. "And we know that God causes everything to work together for the good of those who love God and are called according to his purpose for them" (Romans 8:28, NLT). That promise alone is enough to assure the *believer* that no circumstance between heaven and earth can stop what God has in store for them. For God has fixed in the believers' soul the blueprint necessary for overcoming any problem. Therefor, "I am convinced that nothing can ever separate us from his love" (Romans 8:38a, NLT).

When we encounter Jacob at the brook of Jabbok he is 60 years old, with almost half of his life behind him, and before him the promise that

God had made to him some 20 years earlier, when he said:

"Behold, I am with you and will keep you wherever you go, and will bring you back to this land; for I will not leave you until I have done what I have spoken to you" (Genesis 28: 15, NKJV).

Each of us, having experienced God at some level in our lives, has before us the promise of God's covenant relationship, and the bondage of sin that has colored our memories and crippled our lives. We, like Jacob, are being sent forth by God to embrace the greater blessings that flow from being free from the bondage of our past. That is why Paul said, "…let us lay aside every weight, and the sin which so easily ensnares *us*, and let us run with endurance the race that is set before us" (Hebrews 12:1, NKJV).

What is this "laying aside" that Apostle Paul is referring to? It is the act of allowing ourselves, like Jacob, to be guided over the brook of Jabbok (Genesis 32: 22), to be alone with the silent and sometimes dark truth that God reveals to our hearts. It is coming to a place in our lives where God can begin to do a new work in us. It is the process of sanctification or separation necessary for entry into the next dimension of faith. For here not even wealth, wives, nor children can be allowed to share in the relationship the Lord wants to have with you.

It is a personal encounter with God, and the final confrontation between carnal man and spiritual man. Thus, the child, who once relied so heavily on the nurturing hands of parents, must be separated from them in the continuing progression from childhood to adolescence. This is a critical time in the life of adolescents, and a time when biblical instruction must take on new forms and more thought-provoking experiences. Now more than ever before their bodies are coming alive to the strange sensations of nature, and their souls are restlessly stirring and hungering for relationship with their God. In short, they are entering a *passage* in life where the outside world is colliding with the inside world with almost confusing regularity, and they need to be guided through the process of this sometimes chaotic phase of growth.

Many of the children growing up in our cities are struggling to break free from the restraints placed on them by *others* that have sought to define them. These youth come from households where the father is either a distant memory or a fossil-remain of angry words spewed from the mouth of their mothers. Others have gone from relatives to institutions as they pass through life wondering who they are and where they fit in. Much like Jacob, they want to go home, but fear and a negative self-image stand like a wall ready to impede their steps into the future.

Church leaders need to understand that the boys and girls that move in and out of our society, line our church pews, fill our Sunday School classes, and live in our homes, are struggling to come to terms with *who* they are. They are afraid because they feel isolated by traditional rules of parent-child relationships, and find it hard to believe that adults were once teenagers who experienced life the same way they do. Our youth are terrified by the realization that while Jesus Christ is taught and preached they have never really knew him (like their parents seem to). So they grow up alienated from their homes and strangers in their local churches, passing undetected just below radar, outside our jubilant praises and our planned church revivals. Much like Jacob they never quite meet God, but are sent ahead into life unprepared for what awaits them.

The Genesis writer reports that Jacob did what was typical of most of us when the weight of our sins catches up with us, "he took them and sent them across the brook; also he sent over all that he had" (Genesis 32: 23, NKJV). No matter how noble or well intentioned our actions are as parents, we are often unable to deal with the crisis in our families for having to deal with the personal crisis in us. Thus, until we have surrendered our sins to God we can not once for all deal with the sins crippling our families.

The ironic thing is that we never truly meet God until we reach the point of crisis in our personal lives. That is why Isaiah said, "In the year that King Uzziah died, I saw also the Lord sitting upon a throne, high and lifted up, and the train of His *robe* filled the temple" (Isaiah 6: 1, NKJV). Sometimes, God's light cannot break through the darkness of our minds until the things which we cling to for dear life are put down with a final death blow that hurls them to the sea of forgetfulness. Then we seek first the kingdom of God, and His righteousness (Mathew 6: 33).

The Jacobean Paradox

In order to enter a new dimension of faith we must first make an honest effort to come into the knowledge of God. We must earnestly strive to *practice his presence* or be in relationship with Him. We must fully accept the Good News that Jesus the Christ, the Son of God, the Word of God, the Righteousness of God, is come that we might have "life in all its fullness" (John 10: 10, NLT). We must once and for all be alone with the truth about ourselves: our sinfulness and unworthiness before God, and declare in our souls, "Woe *is* me for I am undone! Because I *am* a man of unclean lips…" (Isaiah 6: 5, NKJV). We must stop judging others and begin to examine ourselves, turning our gaze to heaven in the hour of our being *undone* or *struggling* to break forth from the body of *sin which so easily ensnares us* (Hebrews 12: 1, NKJV). But in that final moment when we are separated from the crowds and the demands of life, and have been left by ourselves to *wrestle* with the remaining fears darkening our hearts, we will, like Jacob, *break through* to the morning!

What is interesting about Jacob's experience at the brook of Jabbok is that the longest period in this three-step rite of passage seems to be when he is alone, and then struggles to come to grips with the fears holding him hostage. We must not fail to appreciate the importance of that, for many of us are crippled and paralyzed by fear, and seem to have been struggling without any sign of a break-through. But the light can break through at any hour in our circumstances, and lift us to heights of unimaginable glory in God. That idea is implied in Genesis 32: 24 by the Hebrew term `âlâh (aw-law), which means *to rise up and break through.* So, if you have found yourself in a struggle, and the hours, days, and months seem long waiting on God to change your situation, just know that, if you are in relationship with God, your struggles are about to give way to a break-through experience in your life. God is about to release enough light into your situation to allow you to face the new challenge that stands waiting to meet you. David said, "Weeping may endure for a night, But joy *comes* in the morning" (Psalms 30: 5, NKJV). So although we don't always know how long our night will be, we do know that joy will eventually break through and shower us with light.

When we look closely at the biblical context in which Jacob appears in Genesis 32:24, we see clearly marked stages that appear to symbolize what I would like to call the Jacobean Paradox: the intricate and sometimes difficult struggle that arises between the Spirit and the flesh. It is the internal battle that rages just beneath the surface of a heated and emotional praise, and even while in the most solemn moments of prayer that struggle attacks our thoughts and distracts us from the center of our worship. That is why Apostle Paul said, "…when I want to do what is right, I inevitably do what is wrong" (Romans 7:21, NLT). "For the flesh lusts against the Spirit, and the Spirit against the flesh: and these are contrary to one another…" (Galatians 5:17a, NKJV).

The term used in Galatians 5: 17 to depict the nature of what goes on between the Spirit and human nature is *epithumé*, to lust, or have a strong desire for. Epithumè is made up of two words epi, in, and thumós, the mind. Epithumè is tied very closely to the activities Apostle Paul took great pains to describe in 2 Corinthians 10: 5b (NKJV), when he said, "…bringing every thought into captivity to the obedience of Christ." After all, it is within the confines of the mind that the battle to gain control over the will and passions of man takes place. It is a battle to win the very soul of man. The importance of understanding what is at stake in this struggle cannot be overstated. I call this struggle the Jacobean Paradox.

The battle to win the hearts and minds of this generation of youth has become increasingly more difficult as the number of young boys finding their way unto court dockets in courtrooms across America is spiraling out of control. Program after program is developed on both the state and federal level in an effort to stem the tide of this crisis. But while these programs have enjoyed limited success, the overall increase in the rate of violent crimes in the average inner city neighborhood is still rising.

One of the implications of this chapter is that the rite of passage is a spiritual period of transition in the life of every person, whether deliberate or incidental. Additionally, that the absence of clear-cut methods for properly guiding individuals in this period will result in serious deficiencies.

Childhood, adolescence, and adulthood should be marked by clear steps to guide individuals through the difficulties of moving from one stage to the next. But more importantly, each stage must be marked by a move from God, or we are left with not much more than the perversities we now witness in every corner of society.

The danger of moving from boys to men without proper direction or guidance from God is insecure, inadequate, boys clothed in bodies that pass for men. For even while Jacob spent 20 years married and fathering children, he never really came into his full maturity until after his encounter with God (at the brook of Jabbok). He was forced to face a past that had kept him prisoner by circumstances he had long outgrown. Like many of us, he had outgrown the place he was in, and the Lord's vision for him was bigger than the vision he had secured for himself.

What happens when God's vision for our lives is bigger than the vision we have for ourselves?

We find ourselves in a constant struggle to at once embrace God's will and simultaneously hold on to the seeming security of our human limitations. That is the nature of the *Spirit lusting against the flesh.*

Leaving Home

I am afraid that we have raised a generation of men whose common ground of identification rests on secular values that have little or nothing to do with God. At best, many of them think sexual conquests and the ability to father children make them men. Still women, who while quite admirable in their attempts to be both mom and dad, have helped to rear boys who never really leave home, but spend countless failed attempts to create "mom" in every woman they meet. While these statements may appear to be oversimplified, I believe there is a basis of support found in three parallel stages of Jacob's life:

(1) The parallel between Isaac marrying Rebekah at 40, years old, and Jacob leaving home at 40, years of age.

(2) The parallel between Rebekah being barren for 20 years and Jacob spending 20 years exiled from home.

(3) The parallel between Isaac being 60 when Jacob was born and Jacob being 60 when he has his encounter with God at the brook of Jabbok.

The parallel between Jacob and Rebekah points to the hope of our deliverance from the separation that stands against the blessings of the Lord. The parallel between Jacob and Isaac points to the long awaited blessing of God, when He spoke to Isaac in Gerar, "Fear not, for I am with you and will favor you with blessings and multiply your descendants for the sake of My servant Abraham" (Genesis 26:24b, Amp.).

The truth of the matter is that Jacob could not become the man God had destined him to be until after he was moved out of his mother's house. That is why the Genesis writer takes great pains to inform us that Isaac loved Esau and Rebekah loved Jacob (Genesis 26:28). It was at the apron strings of his mother that Jacob had begun to be nurtured and matured. And while a mother's care and love are essential for the balanced development of a boy, there is always the danger that a mother's fervent love can sometimes impair the assertive character traits traditionally, not exclusively, attributed to men.

I believe God has deliberately drawn specific parallels between Jacob and his mother throughout the biblical account. Both are left homeless and fruitless in the midst of plenty. They are a constant source of blessing for others, but are themselves in need of a blessing. Twenty years they must labor after their masters, hopeful, faithful, and in constant travail before a God that is never slack concerning His promises. They must be isolated and separated unto God, who alone can quicken their womb. But in blessing them He must cast them out into struggle, and teach them a lesson that is to suffice for all times: God blesses those that wait on him through the struggles (Isaiah 40:31).

The implications here are clear: in order for boys to become men they must be nurtured in a balanced environment that lends itself to those experiences that come from both male and female influences. In those cases, where as today, the male figure is absent from the home, efforts need be made to bring the male under responsible, godly tutelage (Psalms 1:1-2). That point is bore out by the parallel accounts between Jacob and his father, who were both 60 years old when they gave birth to their greatest hope: Isaac brought forth Jacob and Jacob brought forth Israel.

Again, childhood, adolescence, and adulthood should be marked by clear steps that guide individuals through the difficulties of moving from one stage to the next. But more importantly, each stage must be marked by a move from God.

The Church must not allow fear of world opinion to silence it concerning the crisis that is ripping our communities apart. We must not allow the sweep of political correctness to censure our voices (2 Timothy 4:2). We must "earnestly contend for the faith that was once delivered unto the saints" (Jude 1:3, NKJV); we must examine ourselves to see whether we be in the faith (2 Corinthians 13:5); "For the time *has come* for judgment to begin at the house of God…" (1 Peter 4:17, NKJV).

I am convinced that the experiences of Jacob help us to unlock the mystery that seems to allude us concerning the rising tide of violence in America. I see in Jacob a little frightened boy, much like a million others, struggling to come to terms with the realities of selfhood. I see the crippling effects of silent fathers caught in the web of their own failures, and women barren and lost trying their best to bridge the gap left by broken relationships, as they struggle to raise boys into men. I see an economical system that gorges itself on the financial rewards gleaned from shallow men, reared with consumer mentalities, which blind them against other possibilities. I see me, trapped by the limitations of a mind-set that chose to fit in rather than to assume the leadership role of a royal son called to the palace of his Father (John. 1:12; Romans 8:14).

If Jesus Christ is the bridge that gives us access to God, and frees us from the body of sin that lies at the heart of our existence, then it is only in our personal encounter with him that we are able to grow from boys to men. Such is the principles that underlies 2 Corinthians 5: 17 (NKJV), "Therefore, if anyone is in Christ, he is a new creation, old things have passed away; behold, all things have become new."

I pray that in our attempts to raise our children we begin to aggressively move them through each stage of life by clear, biblical principles that truly join them to the body of Christ. I contend with you for the blessing that will infuse old churches with greater zeal and birth new churches wedded to the principles of bold and fervent faith. The kind of faith epitomized at Pentecost when the fire of the Holy Ghost moved the Church into the next dimension of faith. I pray that something in these pages ignites in you a more desperate need to know Jesus our Lord and Savior. Amen.

References

Baxter, J. S. The master theme of the bible: Part 1: the Doctrine of the Lamb. (1973). Wheaton, Ill: Tyndale House.

Birnbaum, P. Jewish concepts. (1964). New York: Hebrew Pub.

Chain-Reference Bible Fifth Imperial Edition. (1998). Indianapolis, IN: B.B. Kirkbride Bible Co.

Hutchinson, O. E. The shameful silence of many black ministers. Online. Available: http://www.hartford-hwp.com/archives/45a/189.htm. Owner-bre-news@igc.org, June 1999.

Life Application Bible: New King James Version. (1993). Wheaton, Ill: Tyndale House.

New Living Bible, New Testament with Psalms and Proverbs. (1996). Wheaton, Ill: Tyndale House.

OJJDP. Statistical briefing book . Online. Available: http:// ojjdp.ncjrs.org/ojstatbb/htm, Sept. 1999.

Ortlund, Jr., C. R. When God comes to church. (2000). Grand Rapids, MI: Barker Books.

Philips, B. J. (1958). Letters to young churches: A translation of the new testament epistles. New York: The MacMillan Co.

Schwartzman, D. Black unemployment: Part of unskilled unemployment. (1997). Westport, CT: Greenwood.

Simmons, D. Black-on-black crime. Online. Available: washtimes.com/twt-print.cfm? December 2002.

Snyder, H. & Sickmund, M. Juvenile offenders and victims. (1999). Washington, D.C. : Office of Juvenile and Delinquency.

The Amplified Bible. (1987). Grand Rapids, MI: Zondervan Pub.

U.S. Department of Justice Bureau of Justice Statistics. Characteristics of homicides in Wisconsin. Online. Available: http:// www.ojp.usdoj.gov/bjs, February 2003.

Wade, T. A new face of women of revelation 12. Online. Available: http:// www.bibleexplained.com/revelation/r-seg11-12/r1209-Eve.htm, January 2003.

Webster's new world dictionary 2n Ed. (1986). New York: Simon and Schuster.

Zodhiates, S. The complete word study dictionary. (1993). Chattanoga, TN: AMG Pub.

About The Author

Gregory L. Grose, preacher, orator, community activist, and youth worker, climbed from the ashes of a past littered by stints in juvenile detention, adult incarceration, drug addiction, and general hopelessness to become one of a rising tide of young Christian leaders laboring in the vineyard of Jesus Christ. He is the founder of Now Faith Ministries, Inc., a nonprofit, faith-based organization, working to address the proliferation of violence and crime in cities across America. He has earned a Bachelor degree in Mass Communication and a Master degree in Business Administration. He is an associate minister at Great Faith Progressive Missionary Baptist Church, in Milwaukee, where Reverend Benjamin L. Nabors, Sr. is pastor.